KU-016-036

Jen is on the beach.
She's standing on the hot sand.
She's waving to her boyfriend, Rick.
Rick and Jen's friends are in the sea.
They are swimming and surfing.

3

Rick is very happy. He has a new surfboard.
The surfboard is red and white.
Rick's favourite sport is surfing.

CENTRAL LIBRARY

MACMILLAN GUIDED READERS

STARTER LEVEL

SARAH AXTEN

Blue Fins

LIBRARIES

INVERCLYDE

MACMILLAN

ORIGINALS

Inverclyde Libraries

34106 002303290

It's hot. The sun is shining. The sky is blue.
The hot sun is shining in the blue sky.

Jen lives in Australia. Jen and her friends
are not at college today. It is the weekend.

Jen walks along the beach. She sits on some rocks.
Jen puts her blue rubber fins on her feet.
She puts the yellow mask and snorkel on her face.

The water is warm. Her blue fins splash loudly.

Jen takes a big breath. She dives under the water. She moves her blue fins and swims very quickly. She goes down and down.

She can see fish and plants. She can see fish and plants through her yellow mask. The fish and plants are very beautiful.

The fish swim all round her. Jen can see yellow fish. She can see blue fish. There are green, red and white fish.

Jen looks at the plants. They grow on the rocks. There are tall plants. There are small plants.

Jen touches the plants. Some plants are soft.
Some plants are hard. Fish live in the plants
and rocks.

Jen sees a sea-urchin. She doesn't touch
the sea-urchin.
It's dangerous. It has sharp spines.

Jen swims up to get air. Her snorkel
comes out of the water. Jen takes a big breath.
She dives down under the water again.

Jen swims past a large rock. Suddenly she stops.
She sees a dolphin. It cannot swim.
The dolphin is in a net.

The net is round the dolphin's body.
The net is round the rocks. The
dolphin cannot swim up to get air.
The beautiful, blue dolphin is dying.

The dolphin moves its fins slowly.
But the net is strong. The dolphin
cannot break the net.

Jen pulls the net from the rocks.
She pulls the net from the dolphin.

The dolphin is out of the net. The
dolphin moves its fins quickly. It swims
fast. The dolphin swims up and up.

It takes a breath of air. The dolphin looks down at Jen. Then it swims away.

Jen is happy. She tells Rick about the dolphin.

11

Next day everybody is swimming. No one is surfing. The sea is flat.

The sun is high in the sky. The hot sun shines on the water. The water is silver and blue.

Men, women and children are in the sea. They are playing and laughing. Everybody is happy.

The lifeguard watches the sea. He looks at the people swimming.

Suddenly, he shouts loudly.

Shark! Quick! Get out of the water!

The shark is swimming quickly. It is hungry. Its black fin is above the water. The shark is swimming towards the people. Everybody is frightened. Sharks are dangerous. They have long, sharp teeth.

Everybody swims towards the beach.

Jen and Rick are swimming a long way from the beach. The shark comes towards Rick. Jen is very frightened. She shouts at Rick.

Rick! Look out!

Rick sees the shark's black fin above the water. The shark is thirty metres away.

Jen and Rick swim towards the beach. Now the shark is fifteen metres away. Jen can see the shark's sharp, white teeth.

Suddenly, they see another fin in the water. A blue fin. It is a dolphin! It is the beautiful, blue dolphin.

The dolphin is swimming towards the shark. The dolphin hits the shark.

The dolphin hits the shark again and again.
The shark swims away. Rick and Jen are safe.